# Got Your Tongue?

### The Real
### Meaning Behind
### Everyday Sayings

# Got Your Tongue?

## The Real Meaning Behind Everyday Sayings

by Daniel J. Porter

illustrated by Donna Reynolds

*For C & K, with love from Dad*

*—DJP*

# CONTENTS

Introduction . . . . . . . . . . . . . . . . . . . . . . .9

Happy as a Clam . . . . . . . . . . . . . . . . . .12

Let's Talk Turkey . . . . . . . . . . . . . . . . .16

Don't Look a Gift Horse in the Mouth . . . .20

Let the Cat Out of the Bag . . . . . . . . . . . .25

Works Like a Dog . . . . . . . . . . . . . . . . . .28

Mind Your P's and Q's . . . . . . . . . . . . . .31

A Baker's Dozen . . . . . . . . . . . . . . . . . .35

A Stitch in Time Saves Nine . . . . . . . . . . .39

Make Hay While the Sun Shines . . . . . . .42

To the Victor Go the Spoils . . . . . . . . . . .47

Hair of the Dog That Bit You . . . . . . . . . .50

Many a Slip Between Cup and Lip . . . . . . .55

Spitting Image . . . . . . . . . . . . . . . . . . .58

No Flies on Me . . . . . . . . . . . . . . . . . . .61

Elbow Grease . . . . . . . . . . . . . . . . . . . .65

His Long Suit. . . . . . . . . . . . . . . . . . . .68

Age-Old Wisdom . . . . . . . . . . . . . . . . .72

Egg on Your Face . . . . . . . . . . . . . . . . .78

Fit as a Fiddle . . . . . . . . . . . . . . . . . . .81

Tongue-in-Cheek . . . . . . . . . . . . . . . . .84

Cat Got Your Tongue? . . . . . . . . . . . . . .87

Maxim Mysteries . . . . . . . . . . . . . . . . .91

# INTRODUCTION

Have you ever heard a saying and wondered where it came from? Do you sometimes hear an expression and find yourself trying to figure out what it means?

For example, if someone were to tell you it's best to *work like a dog* or to *make hay while the sun shines* so that you'll be *happy as a clam,* would you know what he was talking about?

How about if a friend told you it's a good idea to *mind your p's and q's* and not *let the cat out of the bag* because *there's many a slip between cup and lip.* Would that mean anything to you?

Imagine someone asked, "Could you *talk turkey* if the *cat got your tongue?*" What would you tell her?

If you're not certain exactly what

these sentences mean, you've come to the right place! Throughout this book we're going to tackle the mysteries behind the everyday sayings we call maxims. Usually, maxims are familiar expressions that we hear often in our daily lives.

Many of these sayings contain "words of wisdom" passed on to us by people who have dealt with the same kinds of issues facing us today. Maxims are also used to express an opinion shared by many people. *A watched pot never boils* speaks of the frustration we feel while we are waiting for an event to happen. It seems the more we watch, the longer we wait!

One reason for the popularity of maxims is their ability to express a great deal of meaning in just a few words. For example, when we hear *that's nothing to shake a stick at,* we recognize that the speaker is referring to something of great value.

Maxims can be used in many situations, from giving instructions on how to complete a job to helping us understand how we might get the most enjoyment from our lives. Some maxims are hundreds of years old, while others have come into use more recently.

So get ready to test your knowledge of such common phrases as *elbow grease* and *no flies on me.* You might be surprised to find out where these sayings come from—and what they really mean. Maxims are valuable expressions to learn—after all, if someone sent you to the store for a *baker's dozen,* you wouldn't want to come back with *egg on your face!*

# Happy as a Clam

Have you ever wondered about the phrase *happy as a clam?* Is happiness something you think of when you think of clams? You don't see clams on birthday cards. There aren't any clam-shaped stuffed animals lying around. You don't hear many songs telling about a clam's happy life.

In fact, a clam's life may not really be all that joyful. Clams spend their days in the mud of freshwater lakes or in shallow parts of the sea. They hang out there until someone digs them up and eats them for dinner. By our standards, that's not exactly cause for happiness!

There are other *clam* expressions. *Clam up* is a phrase that refers to a person keeping his or her lips tightly sealed, like the shell of a clam. That phrase makes sense. If your hands are sweaty and cold, people may say you have *clammy hands.* Even that one makes sense since clams *are* cold and a little slimy. But what does it mean if you are *happy as a clam?*

☐ **A.** You have a strong desire for a seafood dinner.

☐ **B.** You enjoy sweating, especially from your hands.

☐ **C.** You enjoy keeping your mouth shut tight.

☐ **D.** You are satisfied with things the way they are.

## Time for a Mud Bath!

Our language is changing all the time. New words are invented, and old words take on new meanings. Sometimes phrases become shortened from their original form. *Happy as a clam* is one of those phrases.

Back in the 1840s, people in the New England region started using the expression *happy as a clam at high tide.* To them it made perfect sense, since at high tide the waters are so deep that clams are pushed farther down into the mud . . . and out of the reach of clam diggers. True happiness!

So if you're happy as a clam, **you're satisfied with things the way they are** (D). Either that or you get a kick out of playing in the mud.

### What Do You Call a 500-Pound (225-Kg) Clam?

A King, what else? King clams are the largest clams known. They live in the great coral reefs of the Indian and Pacific oceans and can grow to weigh 500 pounds (225 kg)!

# Let's Talk Turkey

An interesting invitation, don't you think? "Hey, everybody, let's get together and talk turkey!" It would make for a strange-sounding party!

What do you think is meant by *Let's talk turkey?*

☐ **A.** Let's get together and discuss our plans for Thanksgiving dinner.

**B.** Let's make cackling noises by warbling through the loose skin under our necks.

**C.** Let's talk seriously and honestly, getting right to the heart of the problem.

**D.** Let's attract birds, as with "duck calls."

## Turkey Talk

Lean your head about halfway back and pull gently on the skin under your chin. When you've done this, try to make a sound somewhere between a rooster crowing and gargling. Repeat this process rapidly.

If you followed the direction above, your friends might think you look funny, but you would not be "talking turkey." In fact, only when you **talk seriously and honestly, getting right to the heart of the problem** (C), are you "talking turkey."

According to the *Dictionary of Clichés*, the saying *Let's talk turkey* was popularized in the late 1800s by a tale about a Native American and a settler who were hunting together. After the hunt, they began dividing everything they had killed. The settler made sure that every time it was his turn to receive part of the catch, he chose a turkey. When they were finished, the Native American had no turkeys. The settler declared the day a success—until the Native American disagreed, saying, "Not until we talk turkey!"

Today we use the phrase when we want to focus our conversation on an important topic. For example, your parents may want to talk turkey with you about your grades after they review your report card.

# Don't Look a Gift Horse in the Mouth

Most people live by a crazy little rule that seems to say something like: "Never put your head into the mouth of a large animal." Sounds like a fairly sensible idea, doesn't it? It could easily be added to the list of safety tips everyone should know. For example:

**1.** Cross at the green, not in between.
**2.** Never get into a stranger's car.
**3.** Never pet dogs you don't know.

Most people wouldn't even look *at* an animal's mouth, let alone *in* it! The animal might confuse you with its dinner!

Besides the obvious message about safety, what else do you think *Don't look a gift horse in the mouth* means?

☐ **A.** Accept the gifts you are given graciously, without asking how much they cost or what they are worth.

☐ **B.** Never get too close to the person giving you a gift, in case he or she has really bad breath.

☐ **C.** When speaking to someone, look at his eyes and not at his teeth.

■ **D.** Never accept horses as gifts if you don't own a stable.

## Open Wide ...

Did you know you can check a horse's age by looking at his teeth? It's true. If a horse's teeth angle outward and are worn on the surface, it's a sign the horse is relatively old. If the teeth are more vertical, the horse is young.

Before the days of cars, trucks, tractors, and trains, a horse was a very valuable animal to have, and, of course, a young horse was worth more than an older one. If someone was given a horse as a present, it was thought to be very rude to look into the animal's mouth to check its age. It would be like asking someone how much she paid for the gift she was nice enough to give you.

*Don't look a gift horse in the mouth* means that you should **accept the gifts you are given graciously, without asking how much they cost or what they are worth** (A).

Although horses are not usually given as gifts today, this maxim can still have meaning for us. It reminds us that we should take advantage of the opportunities that may come our way without questioning them.

**Horse Power**

Have you ever heard the term "horsepower"? Do you know what it means? It is a unit of measure that reflects how much an engine works compared with a horse's effort. Scientists determined that the average workhorse can move 22,000 pounds (9,900 kg) one foot (.91 m) every minute. To get an idea of how much work that is, think about the fact that 22,000 pounds (9,900 kg) is roughly the weight of ten mid-sized cars! If you hitched those ten cars to an average workhorse, it could pull the cars one foot (.91m) every minute. If an animal is that strong, it's probably a good idea not to look in its mouth!

# Let the Cat
# Out of the Bag

If you have a cat, or if you know someone who does, you probably know that these animals enjoy playing in all sorts of places. Cats have a reputation for enjoying mischievous play and finding secret hideaways. If you talk to cat owners you soon find out that some cats like playing in laundry baskets, others enjoy hiding out in closets, while still others seem particularly fond of hopping into bags.

Does knowing how cats like to play help you figure out this maxim?

To *let the cat out of the bag* means:

☐ **A.** To reveal a secret.

☐ **B.** To perform an act of kindness.

☐ **C.** To help a cat escape. (Before there were pet stores, cats were sold in bags at the market. When you got home you "let the cat out of the bag.")

☐ **D.** None of the above.

## Here, Kitty Kitty

Today, farmers' markets are places where farmers sell produce picked fresh from the fields. But, in days gone by, farm equipment and farm animals were brought to market. Pigs were often sold in bags. Sometimes, in order to keep a valuable pig, a farmer would place a cat in the bag in place of the pig. When the unsuspecting farmer arrived home and opened the bag, he discovered that he'd been tricked.

Today we use this maxim as another way of saying that **a secret has been revealed** (A).

# Works Like a Dog

Dogs are beautiful animals. They make wonderful pets. They play with us, fetch things for us, and some even guard our homes. But when's the last time you saw a dog take out the trash? Have you ever seen a puppy wash dishes? Sweep the floor? Leave for work in the morning with a lunch bag or a briefcase? So what does *works like a dog* mean?

☐ **A.** Panting heavily while working with one's tongue hanging out.

☐ **B.** Digging with one's hands, like a dog who is burying a bone.

☐ **C.** Working hard and steadily, all day long.

☐ **D.** Working in circles, like a dog who is chasing its tail.

## It's a Dog's Life

Before dogs became popular as household pets, they were often used as work animals, particularly as herd dogs to keep a group of cattle or sheep all moving together in the same direction. When an animal drifted away from the herd, the dog would chase it until it went back into the group. It was a job that lasted from sunup to sundown. Some breeds of dogs, such as border collies, are still used today as herd dogs on farms and ranches.

So, if you *work like a dog*, it means you **work hard and steadily, all day long (C)**.

# Mind Your
# P's and Q's

The alphabet has twenty-six letters. Why do you think the letters *p* and *q* were singled out for the saying *Mind your p's and q's?* Why don't people say, "Mind your b's and d's"? The letters b and d look very similar if you glance at them quickly.

What does *Mind your p's and q's* really mean?

☐ **A.** You should not interfere with someone else's business.

☐ **B.** You should learn the alphabet.

☐ **C.** You should look over your work to make sure you haven't made any mistakes.

☐ **D.** You should watch your spelling.

## Where Did My Q Go?

There are two stories that can help us understand where *Mind your p's and q's* came from and what it means. They happened about the same time in history, and they both illustrate that the maxim means **you should look over your work to make sure you**

**haven't made any mistakes** (C).

One of the stories goes back to the time when people would buy produce and other supplies at a local market. In those days the store owner kept a bill, or "tab," of each customer's spending that listed the items purchased. A "q" meant quart, and a "p" meant pint. Since quarts are bigger and more expensive than pints, people warned each other to check their grocery bills closely and would say, *Mind your p's and q's.*

The other story is based on the fact that every word in a newspaper used to be set in place by hand, letter by letter. A typesetter laid out the letters, which were called "type," in rows. If a typesetter wasn't careful, a *q* could look like a *p* and a *p* could look like a *q* (not to mention *b*'s and *d*'s!).

## Now That's a Lot of Typesetters!

Imagine how long it took typesetters to arrange all the words in a newspaper when they did it by hand! No wonder the paper came out only once a week! Did you know that today's desktop computers can put together more than 50 million letters per second?

# A Baker's Dozen

Why is this a popular saying? A certain nursery rhyme mentions a butcher, a baker, and a candlestick maker. Why don't we ever hear about "a butcher's dozen"? Or even "a candlestick maker's dozen"?

When someone says "a baker's dozen," many people may automatically think of sweet treats. If someone said "a farmer's dozen," you might think of a dozen eggs or a dozen chickens. But no one says "a farmer's dozen." Let's consider what's so special about *a baker's dozen.*

■ **A.** A famous banker named John Baker had twelve children. Anyone with twelve children is said to have *a baker's dozen.*

■ **B.** *A baker's dozen* refers to something more than you expected. A baker's dozen has thirteen items, not twelve.

■ **C.** *A baker's dozen* refers to twelve pieces of pastry—just as "a butcher's dozen" refers to twelve pieces of meat and "a plumber's dozen" means twelve toilets!

**D.** *A baker's dozen* refers to a contest in which twelve bakers competed to make the best pastry for the king. Each baker entered twelve baked goods.

## I Demand a Recount!

In 1266 the English Parliament (a parliament is a type of government) listened to the citizens, who were complaining about the cost of bread. Some bakers were shrinking the size of a loaf of bread, but the price stayed the same! In order to make things fair, Parliament enacted a law that defined the exact size and weight for a loaf of bread and all other baked goods.

To put some "teeth" in their law, Parliament also imposed very expensive fines if any baker's breads or pastries were found to be too small or light. Bakers, in fear of being fined, began putting extra amounts in everything. So, *a baker's dozen* **refers to something more than you expected. A baker's dozen has thirteen items, not twelve** (B).

Many people today know that *a baker's dozen* refers to thirteen items, but not many people know the maxim originated more than seven hundred years ago!

# A Stitch in Time Saves Nine

Here's a "maxim mystery" that may leave you scratching your head in wonder. *A stitch in time saves nine.* Saves nine what? People? Animals? Baseball players? What happens if the stitch *isn't* in time—then what?

Can you guess the meaning of this maxim?

■ **A.** A tailor's term for doing a good job.

■ **B.** Solve a problem when it's small to avoid more work later.

■ **C.** A baseball saying, meaning a strikeout.

■ **D.** All of the above.

## A Needle and Thread, Please

The experts have a difficult time agreeing on the origin of *A stitch in time saves nine*. Most believe it came into use within the past hundred years. Many experts also think it is a close cousin to the saying *an ounce of prevention is worth a pound of cure.* Both sentences advise us that it is better to **solve a**

**problem when it's small to avoid more work later (B).**

The use of "nine" in this phrase was probably chosen because it nearly rhymes with "time" and serves to make the phrase more memorable.

# Make Hay While the Sun Shines

When you first hear this maxim, its meaning seems pretty clear. *Make hay while the sun shines* sounds like plain old common sense! It's almost like telling someone to make snowmen in the snow! But maybe there's a mystery lurking somewhere in this saying.

Do you think this maxim has a

hidden meaning? Read the choices below, then read on to see if you're right.

■ **A.** You have to make hay while the sun shines because you can't make hay by the light of the moon, no matter how brightly it shines!

■ **B.** You can't make hay in the rain.

■ **C.** When you make hay, you need a few days for it to dry. So, when you make hay, you have to choose a time when the sun is expected to shine for several days in a row.

■ **D.** Make the most of your chances while you have them.

■ **E.** Both C and D are correct.

## Rain, Rain, Go Away

Maxims often have more than one meaning. They can give instructions for chores and jobs that *must* be done in a certain way; they can also give us good advice on how to make the most of our lives. *Make hay while the sun shines* is one of those maxims having two different meanings. That's why **both C and D are correct** (E).

(C) When you make hay, you need a few days for it to dry. A farmer who is planning to cut a crop of hay down must choose a time when the sun will be shining for several days. This ensures that the hay will be completely dry by the time bailing begins. If the hay becomes wet during the bailing process, it can grow mold—and moldy hay will make farm animals sick. Another danger from wet hay is that it can get very hot, and it may catch fire while drying out.

(D) is also correct because if farmers don't make hay when they have the chance, they and their animals might be in big trouble. Farmers and ranchers know very well that they must work their hardest when the weather gives them the opportunity.

We can learn from the farmers and ranchers to make the most of our chances when we get them. Many maxims advise us that focusing our energy in the present moment is the best and surest way to success and happiness!

## "Hey, That's a Lot of Hay!"

Have you ever wondered how much hay it takes to feed our animals and livestock? Each year, American farmers and ranchers plant 60 million acres (24 million hectares) of hay, and they harvest 157 million tons (143 metric tons) of it to feed their animals! Just think of how much water it takes to wash all that hay down!

# To the Victor Go the Spoils

We know the word *victor* means "winner." The victor of a contest is the person who won. How would you like to be in a contest where the winner gets everything that's spoiled?

"Congratulations! You won! Your prize is all the rotten eggs and sour milk you want! After all, *To the victor go the spoils!*"

What do you think this maxim means?

◻ **A.** In the old days, when the king held a contest, the winner got to take home all the extra food, and some of it was usually spoiled.

◻ **B.** Another meaning of the word *spoils* is "treasures" or "valuables." When a war was won long ago, the victor took all the valuable treasures.

◻ **C.** Once, after a contest held by King Arthur, it was discovered that one of his knights had won by cheating. Instead of giving him a prize, the king made him eat spoiled food and drink spoiled wine.

◻ **D.** *Spoiled* can mean that a person

has been given too many things. When the prize awarded in a contest is too large, the winner is thought to be "spoiled."

## Moldy Meat, Anyone?

When we hear a word, the most common meaning of that word usually comes to mind. To most of us, *spoils* refers to things that have gone bad. We don't want to smell them—and we sure don't want to taste them!

But *spoils* has several meanings. One of them explains the significance of this maxim. **Another meaning of the word *spoils* is "treasures" or "valuables." When a war was won long ago, the victor took all the valuable treasures. (B) is the right answer.**

# Hair of the Dog
# That Bit You

This maxim sounds as if it came from a witch's recipe book: "One eye of a newt, one tail of a lizard, and a little hair of the dog that bit you."

Maybe *hair of the dog that bit you* is about being so angry over a dog bite that you decide to bite the dog back!

Imagine the following conversation

taking place between two good friends:

"What's that in your teeth, Jack?"
"Oh, that? It's just a little bit of
  the hair of the dog that bit me."
"How did you get it in your teeth?"
"I bit him back!"

What do you think this maxim really means?

☐ **A.** It's part of an old forgotten nursery rhyme.

☐ **B.** It means to try something for a second time, even though your first try didn't go very well.

☐ **C.** The hair of a dog that had bitten someone was once used to help heal the bite wound caused by the dog.

□ **D.** Both B & C are correct.

## A Little Off the Top, Please

Maybe you've heard this maxim before and are pretty sure it means **to try something for a second time, even though your first try didn't go very well**—like getting back on a horse after you fall off.

If that's the answer you chose, you wouldn't be wrong, but you wouldn't be totally right either! It turns out that long ago people actually did use the hair of the dog that bit them **to help heal the bite wound caused by the dog**. They would snip some of the dog's hair, burn it, and apply it to the wound. So (D) is the right answer because **both B and C are correct.**

This saying has been around for a long time because people have always had the inclination to keep trying until they get something right. For example, most of us know that Ben Franklin discovered electricity, but perhaps you didn't that know he attempted his famous kite experiment *nineteen* times before he was successful.

## Human's Best Friend

Did you know that dogs have been kept as pets for more than 10,000 years? One of the first references to a pet dog can be found in writings that date back to 8,500 B.C.

The smallest pet dogs are Shih Tzus. They are only 8 inches (20 cm) high and weigh 15 pounds (6.7 kg). Great Danes are the largest dogs. Some full-grown adults measure 37 inches (94 cm) high and can weigh as much as 200 pounds (90 kg). How would you like to try getting some of that dog's hair to heal a bite wound!

# Many a Slip Between Cup and Lip

This is a great example of how words can be combined to produce a vivid mental image to correspond to an idea that is being expressed verbally. When you read this phrase, you might recall an awful experience when you dumped a glass of juice all over yourself.

Like many maxims, this saying has meaning beyond the immediate image that comes to mind when we hear the phrase.

What does *Many a slip between cup and lip* mean?

☐ **A.** It was a World War II slogan that warned people against discussing any military plans.

☐ **B.** It's an advertisement for a straw company. "Drinks go down better with straws because there's many a slip between cup and lip!"

☐ **C.** Things don't always go as planned.

☐ **D.** Many people have accidents while enjoying a beverage, so be careful when drinking your milk.

## Pardon Me

The phrase *Many a slip between cup and lip* has been around for thousands of years. Some experts date its use as far back as ancient Greece!

Perhaps you've even used this phrase. A freak thunderstorm may have dampened your plans for a picnic. Or maybe you were set to go to the mall but your parents got tied up on the phone, so you didn't go. At such times we use the saying *Many a slip between cup and lip* to express the idea that **things don't always go as planned** (C).

As for the World War II slogan mentioned in choice (A), that was *Loose lips sink ships*. This saying cautioned people against speaking about military plans, just in case an enemy spy might be listening!

# Spitting Image

The word *spitting* brings many images to mind, and none of them are very pleasant. Baseball players often spit saliva or tobacco juice out of their mouths during games. When outdoor cooks roast meat over a campfire, the rod they place the meat on is called a spit. Is that what this maxim refers to? What do you think *spitting image* means?

**☐ A.** The phrase is really "splitting image" and means splitting something down the middle so both sides look exactly the same.

**☐ B.** It means finding the shapes of animals or other images in spit.

**☐ C.** It's the reflection you see in "spit-shined" shoes.

**☐ D.** It refers to things or people that look exactly the same.

## Mind Your Manners!

Long ago the phrase *spitting image* referred to a son who looked so much like his father, it was said that the boy had been "spit from his father's mouth." Over time, the expression was altered and modified to "spit and image of his father," and then to *spitting image,* which today **refers to things or people that look exactly the same** (D).

# No Flies on Me

Maxims are repeated over and over again and become part of our everyday language because people *like* to use them. Someone, somewhere, was the first person to use the phrase. Other people heard it, liked it, and began imitating it. What is it about *no flies on me* that people liked? What does it mean?

**A.** I am clean; there are no germs on me. There are no flies on me, either.

**B.** I'm aware of what is going on around me.

**C.** It's a common phrase among horse ranchers, who, after working with horses all day, sometimes have flies stuck to them.

**D.** A camper's bedtime checklist: "Have any snakes on you?" "Have any mosquitoes on you?" "How about flies? Any flies on you?"

## I Don't Need Bug Repellent!

If there are no flies on you, you chose **(B)** because **you're aware of**

**what's going on around you**. If you chose a different answer, you may want to check for pesky flies that might be making a home somewhere on your body!

This phrase no doubt originated in farming communities. Many times a phrase becomes popular after it is printed in a publication of one kind or another. For example, a politician, sports figure, or entertainer may be quoted in a paper or magazine, and within weeks the phrase he or she used becomes part of our everyday lives. Phrases like *Get real, No way,* or *Get a life* color our lives because we hear them on television or read them in the paper.

In 1888 the *Detroit Free Press* published the phrase *no flies on him.* Since then, people have used this maxim to refer not only to themselves but also to others, and it is now a part of our cultural vocabulary.

## Did You See That Fly?

Did you know there are more than 80,000 different kinds of flies?

Did you know the eye of a fly is composed of more than 4,000 facets?

We may not always know where flies are, but with that many parts to their eyes, it's no wonder the flies know where we are!

# Elbow Grease

You can probably imagine that auto mechanics have a tough time keeping grease off their elbows. They work on cars all day long, leaning on the engines as they work—so they're bound to get grease on their elbows, right? Is that what this maxim means? Or maybe elbow grease is used by plumbers to help join all those elbow-shaped pipes under the sink and toilet.

Can you see how tricky it is to try and figure out the meaning of some maxims? If you go just by the words, sometimes you miss the larger meaning! What does *elbow grease* really mean?

**A.** Rare fluid found in the elbow joints of gorillas and known as a strong cleansing agent.

**B.** Additional effort or vigorous physical labor.

**C.** The sweat on our elbows.

**D.** An ointment used to treat tennis elbow.

## This Is Hard Work

If you ever face a tough cleaning job, don't go looking for the fluid found in a gorilla's elbow—they can get very touchy about that!

The use of the word "grease" in this phrase is a reference to the effect grease can have on machine parts that are difficult to move. Grease is a lubricant that, when applied to certain surfaces, allows smoother and more efficient movement. When you combine that definition with a reference to an elbow, it is a way of saying that **additional effort or vigorous physical labor** (B) is needed to solve a stubborn work problem.

If someone suggests that a problem with which you are grappling needs a little *elbow grease,* he is suggesting you put more muscle into your effort!

# His Long Suit

Many of us know the story of the emperor's new clothes, but do you know what happened the day after the emperor walked around the kingdom in his underwear? He was so embarrassed at having been tricked and at having everybody see him in his underwear that from then on he wore a suit long enough to cover every inch of his body! It even flowed down on the ground behind him! The outfit became known as "his long suit."

Do you think the maxim *his long suit* comes from the story about the emperor's clothes? Choose one of these explanations:

☐ **A.** It's an outfit worn by a king or emperor.

☐ **B.** It refers to something that gives you trouble or trips you up—like wearing a suit that's too long for you.

☐ **C.** When you're playing cards, it's the suit in which you have the most cards.

☐ **D.** It's something at which you excel.

☐ **E.** Both C and D are correct.

# Don't Step On My Sleeves!

Suits are sets of clothing. The word *suit* also refers to the groupings of clubs, hearts, spades, and diamonds within a deck of playing cards. We call these groupings suits.

In many card games, having a lot of cards of the same suit translates into controlling the action of that round, or game. You are using *your long suit* to play well. From this origin the phrase expanded to mean "talent." If you excel at something—be it sports, academics, music, making people laugh—your strong talent is considered *your long suit*.

Because the saying keeps its original meaning, the answer is (E) **both C and D are correct.**

## Playing Cards Is Against the Law

Card playing became a popular pastime in Europe in the 1300s. Some cards were shaped like circles, some were large rectangles, some were squares. Other early decks of cards had pictures of creatures from fables, and still others had pictures of the king and his court. By 1397, playing cards had become so popular in France that a law was created to stop people from enjoying this pastime during working hours!

# Age-Old Wisdom

Now that you've learned more about maxims, quiz your friends. See if they know the sayings listed below—and what they mean! People are often surprised to learn the real meaning behind things we say every day.

For a real test of maxim knowledge, ask which of the following maxims is the oldest. Do you know? (The answers follow.)

☐ **A.** That's the way the cookie crumbles.

☐ **B.** Leave no stone unturned.

☐ **C.** I can feel it in my bones.

☐ **D.** Lend me your ears.

☐ **E.** In a nutshell.

☐ **F.** How do you like them apples?

☐ **G.** So far, so good.

**You Don't Say!**

You might be surprised to find out exactly how old some of these age-old sayings are!

A. *That's the way the cookie crumbles.* This saying, which means that things that happen are often decided by chance, is thought to refer to the unpredictable way a cookie breaks. This is the youngest (and tastiest!) phrase of the group, being only forty to fifty years old!

B. *Leave no stone unturned.* This expression, which refers to searching everywhere for a lost item, is more than 2,475 years old! According to legend, this saying was first used by a Greek named Polycrates when he was searching for the treasures of the King of Persia, whom he had defeated in battle.

C. *I can feel it in my bones.* If you study our language and the phrases we use, you soon find out many important contributions were made by an author by the name of William Shakespeare. This saying, which means "to have a premonition, intuition, or hunch" was first used in a play written by Shakespeare called *Timons of Athens*. It appeared in print more than 435 years ago!

D. *Lend me your ears*. Another saying originated by Mr. Shakespeare! This expression, which asks people to listen closely to a speaker, appears in the play *Julius Caesar* and is only a few years younger than the quotation we noted in (C). This one is more than 430 years old!

E. *In a nutshell*. We hear this phrase used when a person is summarizing many facts or comments into a short sentence. The first known use of this saying is in a book called *Natural History*, which was written more than 2,000 years ago!

F. *How do you like them apples?* This is a popular phrase in many farming communities. It was widely used in the 1930s and was meant to compare two items to each other. It became a common phrase after it appeared in 1961 in a play called *The American Dream*, which was written by Edward Albee.

The meaning of this saying has changed a bit over time. Now when someone says *How do you like them apples*, it is usually meant to try and gauge if a person is satisfied with a result or situation.

G. *So far, so good.* This is an easily understood maxim indicating that plans are going well and a project is progressing smoothly. When the English novelist Samuel Richardson first wrote this phrase in 1753, he probably had no idea that his maxim would be so well liked that people still use it more than 245 years later!

# Egg On Your Face

Is that egg on your face? Or is it peach jelly? No, wait, it kind of looks like butterscotch topping. What did you have for breakfast anyway?

And what does *egg on your face* mean?

☐ **A.** Part of a skin treatment. Eggs have many vitamins, and putting eggs on your face is very healthy for your skin.

**☐ B.** In the old days, if you were found to be a liar, several eggs were broken over your head; you had to sit in front of everyone while the yolk ran down your face.

**☐ C.** It means you're embarrassed.

**☐ D.** It's a warning to cooks not to boil eggs too long. The eggs might explode and splash all over the cook's face!

## Scrambled or Fried?

To have *egg on your face* **means you're embarrassed** (C). Wouldn't you be mortified if someone pointed out that you were such a sloppy eater that you had egg on your face?

Although no one knows the exact origin of this phrase, many experts agree that it became popular during modern times because of its widespread use in television comedies and films of the 1950s.

# Fit as a Fiddle

Have you ever heard of a sports team using a fiddle as its emblem?

"We've got a tough game today, team. We're playing the FIDDLES. Now pay attention. They're a noisy bunch, and they can be a little high strung!"

How about a cereal company?

"Eat our Crunchy Flakes, they'll make you fit as a fiddle!"

When you imagine a fiddle's shape,

you don't immediately think of physical fitness—do you?

What does *fit as a fiddle* mean?

▭ **A.** Having a long, skinny upper body and a wide lower body.

▭ **B.** Feeling fit and trim—just like a musical instrument that has a good tone.

▭ **C.** To be proper, to fit into place.

▭ **D.** It's a mean thing to say about someone. It's like saying, "you're as fast as a snail."

## Looking Good

Fiddles were very popular musical instruments in America during the

1800s, and they still are today. Well-made fiddles are prized for their sound and their trim, even shape. The phrase *fit as a fiddle* dates as far back as 1616, but it became popular in America during the late 1800s. People used the maxim to let others know they felt **fit and trim—like a musical instrument that has a good tone** (B).

# Tongue-in-Cheek

Perhaps this maxim came into use during tongue-twister contests. If you mastered such tongue twisters as "Sally sells sea shells by the seashore" and "Peter Piper picked a peck of pickled peppers," then you advanced to the next round of competition. In that round you had to repeat the tongue twisters while placing your tongue against your cheek. *Now,* try saying those tongue twisters three times fast!

If you don't think *tongue-in-cheek* was once a tie-breaker for tongue-twister contestants, what do you think it means?

☐ **A.** To speak sarcastically.

☐ **B.** An exercise to do when you are practicing public speaking.

☐ **C.** To speak with your mouth full.

☐ **D.** To slur your words.

## Tongue-in-Cheek

If you've ever tried to speak with your tongue tucked up against your cheek, you know it's not easy to do!

The maxim *tongue-in-cheek* doesn't

actually refer to speaking with your tongue out of place. It originally meant that someone had said something he didn't mean and stuck his tongue in his cheek *after* he said it to signal that he was **speaking sarcastically** (A). It's the same as winking after you say something you don't really mean.

Winking has one advantage over sticking your tongue in your cheek: You have no chance of accidentally biting your eyelid!

## The World's Toughest Tongue Twister

Ready to try the toughest tongue twister in the English Language? Test your skill with this, but please don't try it with your tongue in your cheek:

*The seventh sheik's sixth sheep's sick.*

# Cat Got Your Tongue?

This maxim doesn't present a very pretty picture at all, does it? It's right up there with *hair of the dog that bit you*. Seems like our favorite pets—cats and dogs—aren't spoken of very nicely in these sayings!

How did *Cat got your tongue?* become so popular? Was there once a problem with cats grabbing people's tongues? Imagine the news reports: "The surgeon general has just listed cats as the leading cause of tongue loss in America."

It's enough to make you put your favorite furry feline outside while you sleep. You wouldn't want to wake up without a tongue, would you?

What do you think this maxim is really saying?

■ **A.** A person is unable or unwilling to speak.

■ **B.** A loss of feeling in your body, once caused by certain medicine.

■ **C.** A fear of being whipped for speaking.

■ **D.** All of the above.

## What Did You Say?

Interestingly enough, **all of the above** (D) is the correct answer. None of the explanations is the clear origin of the phrase, so they all share the credit! But today, most people agree the expression means **a person is unable or unwilling to speak** (A).

Long ago there was a medicine known as kat that affected the heart. One of its temporary side effects was that it left those who took it unable to speak. It was said that the "kat got their tongues."

Yet another explanation for the origin of *Cat got your tongue?* comes from a popular whip used in olden days. It was fashioned from nine knotted cords tied to a handle. The cords resembled cats' tails. If someone was afraid of being whipped for misbehaving, people would ask, "What's the matter, the cat got your tongue?"

Now when anyone asks you the meaning of the expressions listed in this book, he or she will find the cat definitely does not have your tongue! You'll be able to speak up loud and clear and explain the answers to the mysteries within the maxims we hear spoken every day!

# Maxim Mysteries

Is there a phrase you've heard that you would like to know more about?

Do you have a favorite phrase you like to use—one that you've made up?

Write to us about your mystery maxim or your own favorite saying. Who knows, maybe someone will be telling *your* story in a book someday! And that's *nothing to shake a stick at!*

In fact, wouldn't that just be the *cat's pajamas? Cat's pajamas?* Now what does that mean?

Send your favorite sayings to:

Daniel Porter
c/o Troll Communications L.L.C.
100 Corporate Drive
Mahwah, NJ 07430

# Look for all the books in the

# 101
Ways
## series

### 101 Ways to Do Better in School
0-8167-3285-X   $2.95 U.S. / $4.25 CAN.

### 101 Ways to Get Straight A's
0-8167-3565-4   $2.95 U.S. / $4.25 CAN.

### 101 Ways to Boost Your Writing Skills
0-8167-3835-1   $2.95 U.S. / $4.25 CAN.

### 101 Ways to Boost Your Math Skills
0-8167-3836-X   $2.95 U.S. / $4.25 CAN.

### 101 Ways to Take Tests with Success
0-8167-4225-1   $2.95 U.S. / $4.25 CAN.

### 101 Ways to Read with Speed and Understanding
0-8167-4226-X   $2.95 U.S. / $4.25 CAN.

### 101 Ways to Boost Your Science Skills
0-8167-4451-3   $2.95 U.S. / $4.25 CAN.

### 101 Spelling Traps and How to Avoid Them
0-8167-4923-X   $2.95 U.S. / $4.25 CAN.

### 101 Ways to Speak in Front of Your Whole Class
0-8167-4917-5   $2.95 U.S. / $4.25 CAN.

### 101 Key SAT Words
0-8167-4938-8   $2.95 U.S. / $4.25 CAN.

# Do you have a minute?

Then take the *One-Minute Challenge*. These books are packed with tricky challenges to test your basic skills in math, English, and vocabulary. With answers in the back of each book, these quizzes are a perfect primer for the SATs. Earn better grades starting today!

**One-Minute Challenges: Math**
0-8167-4077-1     $2.95 U.S. / $4.25 CAN.

**One-Minute Challenges: English**
0-8167-4076-3     $2.95 U.S. / $4.25 CAN.

**One-Minute Challenges: Vocabulary**
0-8167-4227-8     $2.95 U.S. / $4.25 CAN.

**One-Minute Challenges: Math and Reasoning**
0-8167-4228-6     $2.95 U.S. / $4.25 CAN.

# NOTES

# NOTES

# NOTES